Accidental Genius

Science Puzzles for Clever Kids

MOUNTAINS, VALLEYS, RIVERS, and OCEANS

Earth Science

Alix Wood

WINDMILL BOOKS

Photocopy, print, or trace the puzzles if you are sharing this book with others. Then you won't spoil the book for the next person.

Color It In

	1	2	3	4
A				
B				
C				
D				

Published in 2024 by Windmill Books,
an Imprint of Rosen Publishing
2544 Clinton Street
Buffalo, NY 14224

Written, designed, and illustrated by Alix Wood
All other images © AdobeStock Images

Cataloging-in-Publication Data

Names: Wood, Alix.
Title: Mountains, valleys, rivers, and oceans / Alix Wood.
Description: Buffalo, New York : Windmill Books, 2024. |
Series: Accidental genius: science puzzles for clever kids |
Identifiers: ISBN 9781538395288 (pbk.) | ISBN 9781538395295 (library bound) | ISBN 9781538395301 (ebook)
Subjects: LCSH: Earth sciences--Juvenile literature. | Life sciences--Juvenile literature. |
Games--Juvenile literature. | Picture puzzles--Juvenile literature.
Classification: LCC QE501.25 .W66 2024 | DDC 550--dc23

Printed in the United States of America

CPSIA Compliance Information: Batch #CW24WM
For Further Information contact Rosen Publishing at 1-800-237-9932

Find us on

Contents

Our Planet, Earth

Earth is one of eight planets that travel around our Sun. Earth is the only planet we know of that has life on it. Life is possible because Earth is not too hot and not too cold. It has water to drink and oxygen to breathe.

When Earth formed, about 4.5 billion years ago, it was just a ball of swirling gas and dust! The ball cooled and formed a rocky crust. The planet changed a lot over billions of years to be the place we know today.

Our Solar System

Eight planets travel around our sun. Match each planet to its picture below. Then, color the pictures in.

Mercury   Earth   Uranus

Venus   Mars   Jupiter   Saturn   Neptune

the sun

Mercury   Venus   Earth   Mars   Jupiter   Saturn   Uranus   Neptune

Copy this picture first if you are sharing this book.

Earth Is Like an Onion

The Earth is made up of layers. We live on the thin outer layer, known as Earth's crust. The Earth gets hotter as you get closer to the center. Earth's inner core is almost as hot as the surface of the sun!

outer core

inner core

crust

mantle

The Earth's crust is around 21 miles (35 km) thick. It is 3,967 miles (6,385 km) from the surface to the center of Earth's core.

Can you match the label to the right layer of Earth?
Write your answers on a separate sheet of paper.

1. The hot metal inner core is solid. The weight of the rest of Earth is pressing down on it!

2. The mantle under the crust is rocky. Closer to Earth's hot center, the rock melts into liquid.

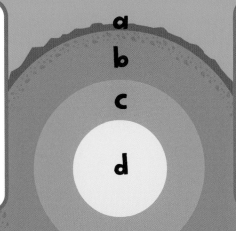

3. The rocky crust is just 1 mile (1.6 km) thick under some parts of the ocean.

4. Earth's outer core is made of metal. The metal is so hot, it has melted into liquid.

Make a Model of Earth's Layers

You will need: modeling clay, a toy knife

1. Make a small ball using one color of modeling clay.

2. Flatten out a circle of different color clay. Wrap the clay circle around the ball.

3. Flatten out a second circle of clay using a third color. Wrap that around the ball.

4. Flatten out a third circle of blue clay. Wrap that around the ball. This is your Earth's crust. You could add some green areas of land.

5. Using a blunt knife, slice your clay ball in half. Can you see all of Earth's layers?

Shifting Land

Earth hasn't always looked like it does now. At first, there was just one big area of land. Very slowly, the land broke apart. The land now forms seven separate continents.

Copy this picture first if you are sharing this book.

Color In the Continents

North America

South America

Europe

Asia

Africa

Australia

Antarctica

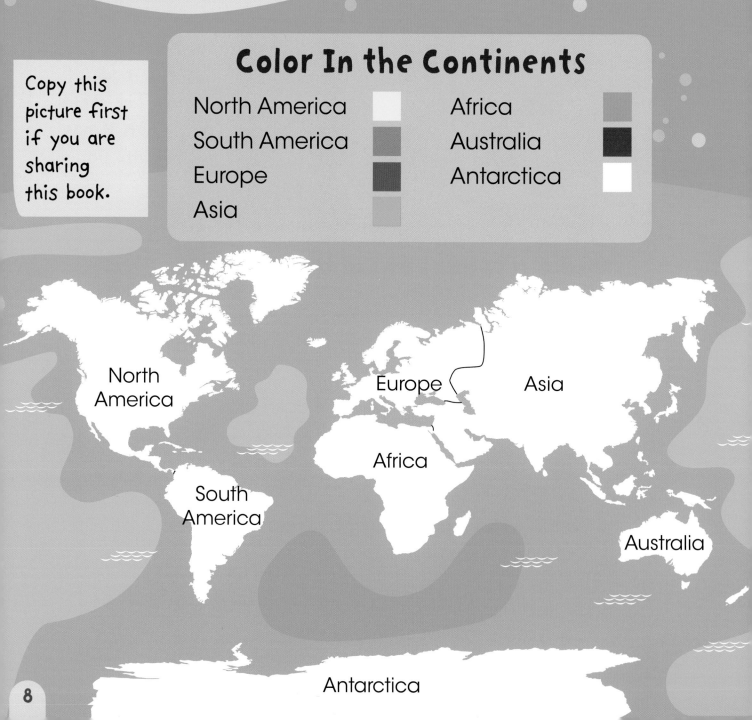

North America

Europe

Asia

Africa

South America

Australia

Antarctica

The land on Earth's crust is always slowly moving. Australia is heading toward Asia. Africa is moving away from Asia, and North and South America are drifting west!

The Earth's crust is made up of several plates. They float on the partly liquid mantle. If the plates move against each other, it can cause the ground to shake!

Unscramble the letters in the circle to find out what the shake is called.

E A R T H __ __ __ __ __

U   A
  E
K   Q

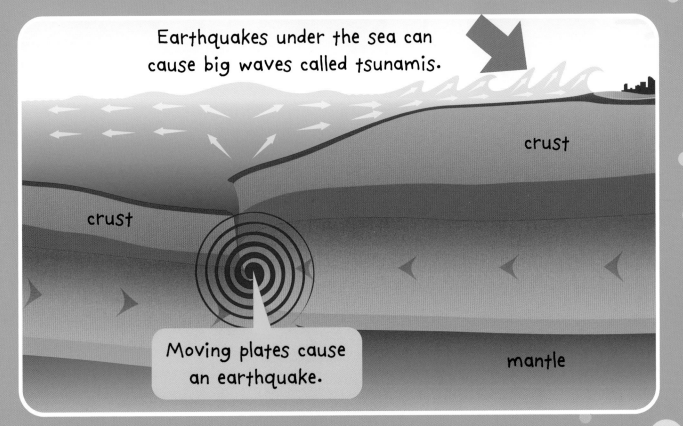

Earthquakes under the sea can cause big waves called tsunamis.

crust

crust

Moving plates cause an earthquake.

mantle

Our Old, Rocky Crust

The Earth's crust is solid rock, covered in small rocks, sand, and soil. Some of the rock was once hot, liquid rock, deep inside Earth. It rose to the surface or was spat out by erupting volcanoes! Other rock was formed by sand, shells, and pebbles that got pressed together.

Granite

When hot liquid rock cools belowground, it becomes grainy like this granite rock.

Sandstone

Rock made from sand and pebbles may have fossils in it, like this sandstone.

Obsidian

When hot liquid rock cools aboveground, it becomes glassy like this obsidian rock.

Can you match each rock to the right label?

1. glassy obsidian from a volcano

2. granite that cooled underground

3. sandstone from a river bed

a

b

c

What Is a Fossil?

Fossils are evidence of a dead plant or animal found in rock. Fossils can be millions of years old. Dinosaur bones, eggs, footprints, and even dinosaur poop have been found preserved in rock!

Fossils form when animals and plants fall into thick mud. Over time, the mud turns to rock in and around the bones, poop, or footprints.

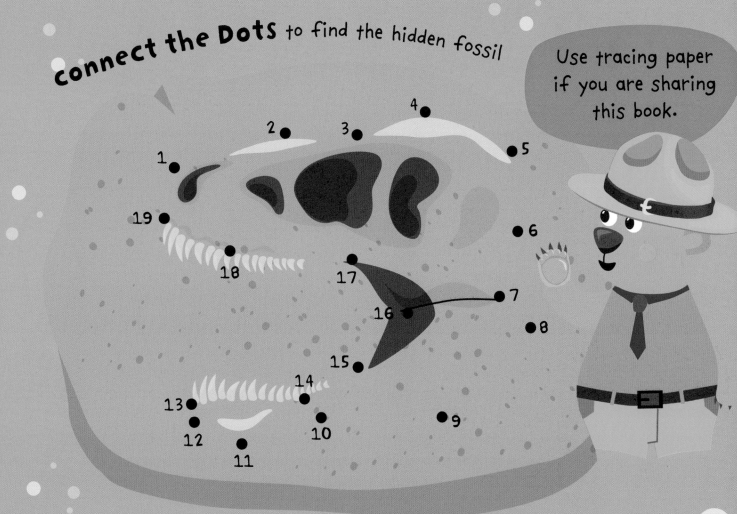

Connect the Dots to find the hidden fossil

Use tracing paper if you are sharing this book.

Thin Crust, Thick Crust

The Earth's crust isn't flat and even. It has thin parts and thick parts. The crust under the ocean is thinnest. The crust in large mountain ranges is the thickest.

Color It In

thin crust

thick crust

mantle

The Himalayas are Earth's highest mountain range. The mountains were created millions of years ago when two plates banged into each other. The crust was thrown up into the air and formed huge mountains! Mount Everest is the tallest.

The highest mountain in the world is in the Himalayas. Write its name on a separate sheet of paper.

E __ __ E __ E __ __

Exploding Volcanoes!

A volcano is an opening in Earth's crust. Volcanoes often occur where plates on the crust meet. When a volcano erupts, hot magma escapes through the opening. The liquid rock is so hot it burns everything in its path! Many mountains, and even whole islands, have been created by erupting volcanoes.

Magma, gas, and ash erupt from deep inside Earth.

Earth has around 1,900 active volcanoes. Active means they are likely to erupt again.

cloud of gas and ash

When magma leaves a volcano, it is called lava.

Most active volcanoes are in a circle around the Pacific Ocean known as the Ring of Fire.

vent

layers of lava and ash

crust

magma

mantle

Can you match each label to the right part of the volcano?

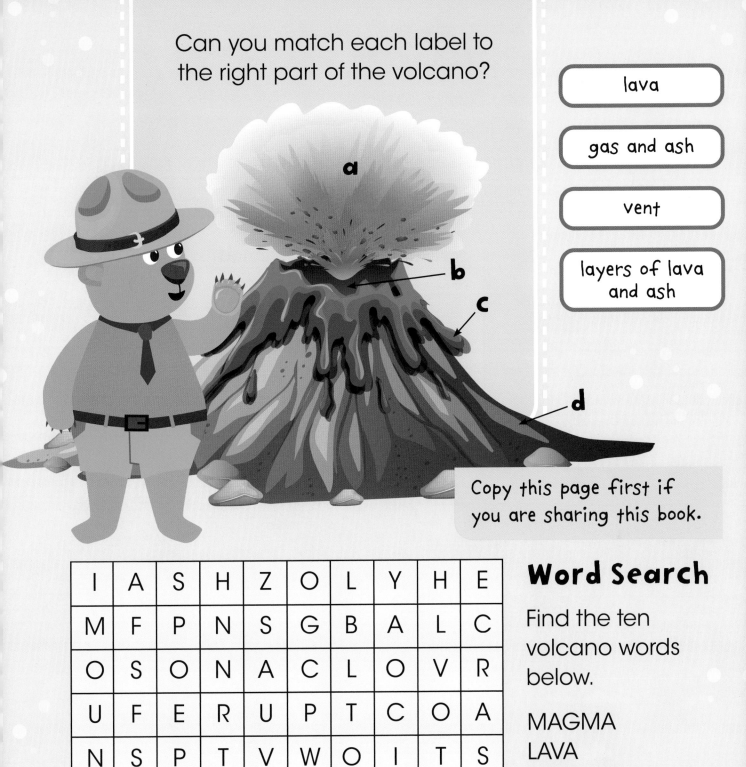

lava

gas and ash

vent

layers of lava and ash

Copy this page first if you are sharing this book.

I	A	S	H	Z	O	L	Y	H	E
M	F	P	N	S	G	B	A	L	C
O	S	O	N	A	C	L	O	V	R
U	F	E	R	U	P	T	C	O	A
N	S	P	T	V	W	O	I	T	S
T	D	C	R	A	T	I	F	E	T
A	H	L	H	M	L	N	I	T	N
I	W	S	A	G	P	P	C	G	E
N	S	P	I	A	E	K	A	H	V
U	L	Q	U	M	V	S	P	R	M

Word Search

Find the ten volcano words below.

MAGMA
LAVA
VOLCANO
ASH
MOUNTAIN
PLATES
ERUPT
PACIFIC
VENT
GAS

Amazing Rivers

Rivers are filled with fresh water. Many animals come to rivers to drink. Reptiles, amphibians, and fish spend some or all their lives in rivers.

Can you find the 8 animals?

frog   fish

pigeon   bear

owl   beaver

fox   wolf

Rivers often start in mountains. Melting snow or rain forms a small stream that runs down the mountainside. The stream gets bigger, until it forms a river. Rivers can also form from underground mountain springs.

Use your finger to find out which of these streams reaches the ocean.

a. the rainy stream

b. the snowy stream

c. the spring stream

the ocean

How Are Valleys Made?

A valley is the low land between hills or mountains. Valleys can be formed by flowing water. As rivers move soil and rock, they carve out a channel. The valley slowly becomes wider as the water moves more and more rock.

Make Your Own Valley

You will need: a clean cat litter tray or any large plastic tub, some sand, pebbles, a jug of water.

1. Pour the sand into one end of the tray.

2. Create a mountain landscape out of the sand. Make one large mountain at the edge of the tray. Form a downward slope toward the empty end of the tray.

3. Scatter some pebbles around your landscape.

4. Slowly pour water onto the tall mountain. Watch what happens.

A river valley should start to form in the sand. The water pulls sand and pebbles along as it flows to the ocean.

Sliding Ice and Moving Plates

U-shaped valleys are formed by huge blocks of ice, known as glaciers. The glaciers pull rock and soil along with them as they slowly slide downhill.

Rift valleys are formed when plates beneath Earth's crust pull away from each another. An area of land drops down between the plates.

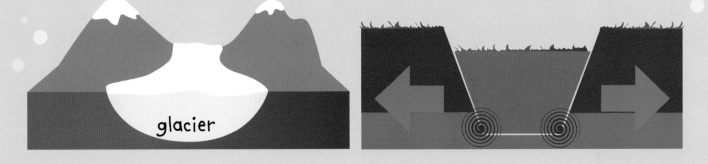

glacier

Copy this picture first if you are sharing this book.

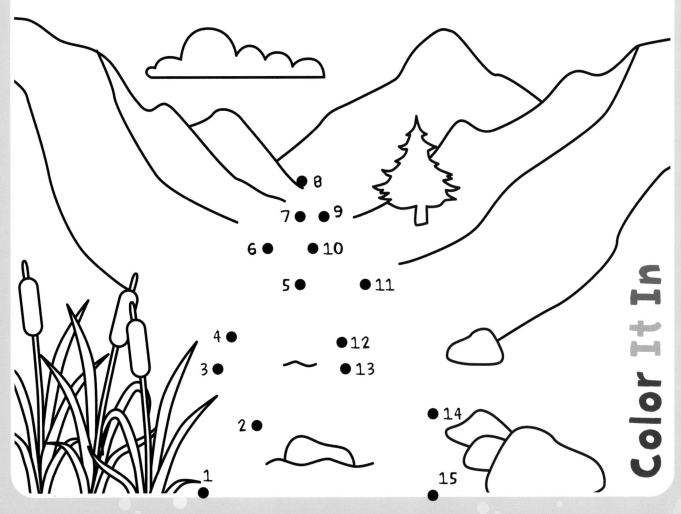

connect the Dots to find what formed this valley.

8
7 • •9
6 • • 10
5 • •11
4 •
3 • •12
~ •13
2 •
•14
1
15

Color It In

Salty Oceans

Around 70 percent of Earth's surface is covered by the ocean. Oceans are full of salty water. Although really there is just one big ocean, we split it into five smaller oceans: the Atlantic, Pacific, Indian, Arctic, and Southern Oceans.

Color It In

Color the oceans blue.   Color the land green.

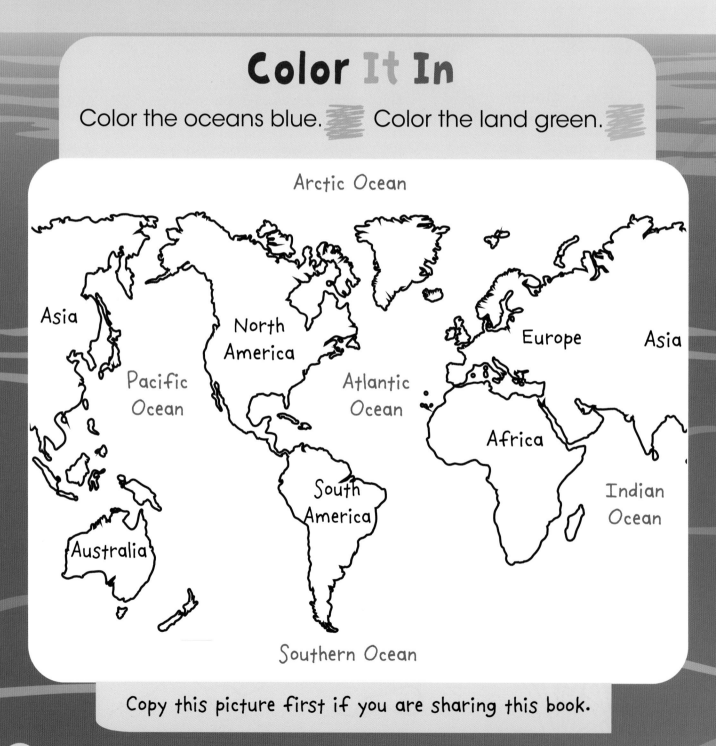

Copy this picture first if you are sharing this book.

Word Scramble

Can you unscramble these letters and find the names of three oceans?

1) R T I A C C _ _ _ _ _ _ _ OCEAN

2) N D I I A N N _ _ _ _ _ _ _ OCEAN

3) P I C F C A I _ _ _ _ _ _ _ _ OCEAN

Did You Know?

The Pacific Ocean is the largest and deepest ocean on Earth. It is bigger than all the land put together!

Can you spot 8 flying birds?

Freshwater Lakes

Lakes are areas of water that are surrounded by land. They are larger than a pool or pond. Most lakes are full of fresh water.

The Great Lakes

Five linked lakes in North America hold the largest single area of fresh water on Earth!

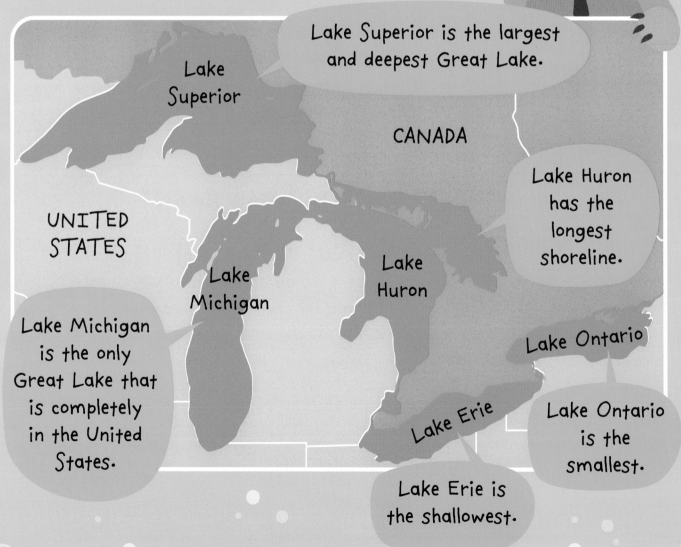

Lake Superior

Lake Superior is the largest and deepest Great Lake.

CANADA

Lake Huron has the longest shoreline.

UNITED STATES

Lake Michigan

Lake Huron

Lake Ontario

Lake Michigan is the only Great Lake that is completely in the United States.

Lake Erie

Lake Ontario is the smallest.

Lake Erie is the shallowest.

Shape Match

Can you match each Great Lake name to its outline?

Lake Erie

Lake Huron

Lake Michigan

Lake Ontario

Lake Superior

Not all lakes have fresh water. The Great Salt Lake in Utah was once a much larger freshwater lake. The water had tiny amounts of salt in it. Hot, dry weather dried up a lot of the water. The water that was left became really salty!

Did you know that salt makes the water denser? It is much easier to float on a saltwater lake than a freshwater lake!

Big, Icy Glaciers

In some cold areas of Earth, old snow gets squashed by the weight of years of fresh snow. The squashed snow becomes ice, and in time forms a glacier. Glaciers are thick masses of ice that move downhill VERY slowly.

Fun on a Glacier!

Glaciers are slippery and icy. Which of these sports could you do on a glacier?

1. Sledding　　2. Skating　　3. Soccer　　4. Skiing

Where Do Glaciers Form?

Glaciers form near the Arctic and Antarctic because those areas get the least amount of sun. Can you find the Antarctic in this picture?

the Arctic

Greenland

sun's rays

Places near the equator are hotter because they get the most direct sun.

Glaciers can form on cold, snowy mountainsides.

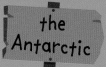

the Antarctic

If all the Antarctic's ice melted, our seas would rise around 213 feet (65 m). That's higher than a 15-story building!

Did You Know?

The Great Lakes were formed by glaciers! Moving glaciers carved dips in the landscape. Then, the melting ice filled the dips with water.

Super Soil!

Much of Earth's surface is covered with a layer of soil. Soil is a mixture of tiny bits of rock, dead plants and animals, air, and water. Most plants need soil to grow. It gives them food and helps root them to the ground. Many animals make their homes in soil, too.

Which two of these grow or live in soil?

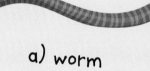

a) worm

b) fish

c) grasses

We need soil to live, too! People eat plants and animals. We would have no food if there were no plants that live in soil, or animals that eat those plants.

Worm Maze

Use your finger to follow the worm holes to find which one ate the apple.

a

b

c

Our Warm Sun

The sun is a bright, burning hot star. Its warmth and light help things grow on Earth. Our spinning Earth takes a year to travel around the sun. Because Earth spins slightly on its side, different parts of Earth lean toward the sun more at some times of the year. That's why we get different seasons.

Countries leaning toward the sun get plenty of sunlight, so it is summer there.

In winter, the same countries lean away from the sun and get less sunlight.

the sun

Earth takes a year to travel around the sun.

Spot the Difference

In winter, the sky turns gray, and snow may cover the ground. Can you find 9 other differences in these summer and winter pictures?

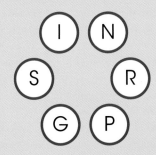

The sun is so bright, it can hurt your eyes if you look straight at it. Wear eye protection on a sunny day.

Unscramble these letters to find the names of Earth's other two seasons.

I N

S R

G P

A L

L F

_____ _____

Super-Useful Plants

Thousands of different plants grow on Earth—from enormous trees, to plants so tiny you can barely see them!

Plants make oxygen. Oxygen is a gas that living things breathe.

Plants provide us and other animals with food.

Medicines, paper, chewing gum, cork, and rubber all come from plants.

We can make clothes from plant fibers.

We build homes using wood from trees.

Flowers can decorate our homes and gardens.

Plants make great animal homes. Can you find the frog?

A Tomato Plant's Life Cycle

1. Seeds form inside the fruit.

2. A seed falls into warm, damp soil.

3. The seed starts to grow.

4. The seedling grows up toward the light.

5. Strong roots hold the plant in the soil.

6. The seedling grows leaves and flowers.

7. The flowers turn into fruit.

Use a separate sheet of paper to put these pictures in the right order to grow a seed into a new tomato.

a

b

c

?
1

?
2

?
3

Underground Caves

A cave is a hole in the rock, under the ground. Most caves are formed where there is soft rock called limestone. As water flows through the cracks, the soft stone wears away. Slowly, the cracks get bigger and form a cave.

Dripping water contains minerals that stick to the cave ceiling and floor. Over the years, the minerals form long spikes.

Spikes that hang from the ceiling are called stalactites.

Spikes that point up from the floor are called stalagmites.

Sometimes the two join to form columns!

Word Search

Find ten animals that might live in a cave.

B	L	S	H	Z	O	L	R	A	T
M	E	P	O	W	L	H	A	L	C
O	S	A	N	A	C	U	O	E	R
E	F	E	R	U	P	R	K	X	F
L	S	P	T	V	R	A	T	G	I
T	D	C	R	E	N	C	F	P	S
E	H	W	D	S	L	C	L	T	H
E	W	I	A	G	R	O	B	A	T
B	P	P	I	A	E	O	A	H	V
S	N	A	I	L	V	N	P	R	M

BAT
BEAR
RACCOON
SNAIL
SPIDER
OWL
BEETLE
SNAKE
FISH
RAT

Caves can be miles long, with linked rooms and tunnels. Mammoth Cave in Kentucky is over 350 miles (560 km) long!

Can you find the bat?

Earth Power

Most machines we use need power to make them run. We create power using things we find on Earth. We can power things using wind, waves, heat from the Sun, or heat from deep inside Earth. We can drill into the ground to find oil, gas, and coal. These create energy when they burn.

Once we burn oil, gas, or coal, they are gone forever. Burning also creates pollution that harms our air and water. We will always have plenty of sunlight, wind, and waves, so these types of energy can't be used up. Energy that can't be used up is called "renewable."

Which of these types of energy are renewable?

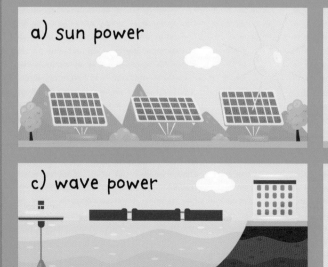

a) sun power

b) coal power

c) wave power

d) wind power

Make Your Own Wind Power!

You will need: some modeling clay, a toothpick, a toilet paper tube, cardstock, a pencil, scissors, a windy day, adult help

1. Draw this windmill blade shape onto cardstock. Carefully cut out your shape.

center toothpick hole

2. Ask an adult to help poke a toothpick through the center of the cutout. Make this hole a little larger by pushing a pencil point into the hole. Then, poke a small toothpick hole near the top of the toilet paper tube.

3. Push some modeling clay onto the end of the toothpick, inside the toilet paper tube. Press the clay so it sticks to the back of the tube.

4. Place the blades on the other end of the toothpick. Use a blob of modeling clay to hold the blades in place.

Take your windmill outside and watch it spin in the wind!

The Sky Above Us

Look up into the sky. What can you see? You might see clouds, or maybe a bird or aircraft flying overhead. The sky around Earth is called our atmosphere. Our atmosphere keeps us warm and gives us air to breathe.

Which of these might you find in the sky?

a

b

c

d

e

f

g

many layers. Using your finger, match each picture to the right layer.

a

b

c

exosphere

The exosphere separates our atmosphere from the rest of space.

thermosphere

The International Space Station travels around in the thermosphere.

mesosphere

Falling meteors burn up when they meet gases in the mesosphere.

stratosphere

the ozone layer

In the stratosphere, the ozone layer protects Earth from the sun's harmful rays.

troposphere

The troposphere is closest to Earth. It contains the air we breathe, and clouds and weather.

Islands

Islands are areas of land with water on each side. Islands are found in rivers, lakes, and oceans. Lake islands can be tiny. Earth's largest island is Greenland. It is surrounded by ocean.

Some islands suddenly appear out of the ocean. How? They are formed when an underwater volcano erupts.

Underwater coral reefs can grow so big, the coral forms an island.

Islands can be manmade. Some concrete islands are used as airports.

Some islands were connected to the mainland long ago. Slowly, water wore away the land and surrounded them.

Island Sudoku

Each red square, row, and column must contain each type of island. Can you find the missing ones?

1.  2. 3. 4.

Can you pick the right bridge to island-hop to the finish?

Start

a

b

c

Finish

How High? How Deep?

How do people figure out which mountain is tallest or which valley is deepest? People need something flat and even to measure things from. Earth's crust is bumpy. Our oceans are the same level all around Earth. So people use "sea level" to measure things from.

The highest point above sea level is Mount Everest, in Nepal.

The highest point measured from the ocean floor is Mauna Kea, in Hawaii.

Tides make the sea bumpy, too. Scientists figure out the average sea level.

Measure from Sea Level

You will need: a ruler

How deep is the underwater trench?
How tall is the mountain?

— sea level ——————————

Can you match the labels to the right feature?

ocean ◯   river ◯

mountain ◯   hill ◯

valley ◯   lake ◯

Can you find the seal in the picture?

Caring for Earth

We need to look after our planet. Our plastic trash harms sea life in the oceans. Burning fuel harms our atmosphere. Changing just a few of the things we do every day can make a big difference.

You Can Help!

Try these tips to help save the planet.

1. Go on a trash hunt. Wear gloves, and ask an adult to help. Put any plastic in a trash bag. Recycle any plastic you can and throw the rest in the garbage. Every piece you pick up may help save an animal's life.

2. Make your yard a wildlife haven. Build a bee hotel, make a log pile, or create a pond. If you have an outdoor cat, put a bell on its collar so wildlife can hear it coming. Small mammals and frogs will thank you!

3. Do all you can to save power and save water. Shut off the faucet while you brush your teeth. Switch off lights when you leave a room.

Easy Steps to Save the Planet!

Copy the drawing in each square into the correct square in the grid below. What did you draw?

A 1   A 2   A3   A4   B 1

B 2   B 3   B4   C1   C2

C3   C 4

Trace the grid onto some paper if you are sharing this book.

We have filled in the first square for you.

	1	2	3	4
A				
B				
C				

Color It In

Try walking instead of taking the car.

Earth Genius Test

Are you a planet Earth genius? Answer these questions to find out.

1 Which layer of Earth do we live on?

a) the mantle

b) the crust

c) the inner core

2 Which of these is not the name of an ocean?

a) the Pacific   b) the Atlantic   c) the Himalayas

3 How do people measure mountains that are on land?

a) They fly over them in a plane.

b) They measure them from sea level.

c) They use the sun.

4 Which of these things do we get from plants?

a) food to eat

b) fiber to make clothes

c) oxygen to breathe

d) all of these things

5 Renewable energy, like sun and wind power, can't be used up. Which of these types of energy is NOT renewable?

a) coal

b) sunshine

c) wind

Answers

Page 7:
1) d 2) b 3) a 4) c

Page 9: EARTH**QUAKE**

Page 10: 1) b 2) c 3) a

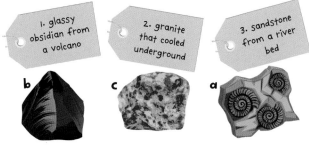

Page 11:
a dinosaur skull

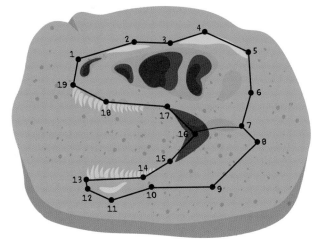

Page 13:
Mount EVEREST

Page 15 top: a = gas and ash,
b = vent, c = lava, d = layers of lava
and ash

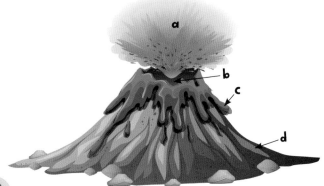

Page 15 bottom:

Page 16:

Page 17: b

46

Page 19: A river formed the valley.

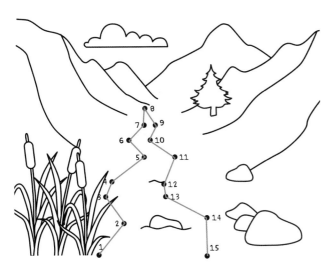

Page 21: 1) Arctic Ocean 2) Indian Ocean 3) Pacific Ocean

Page 23:

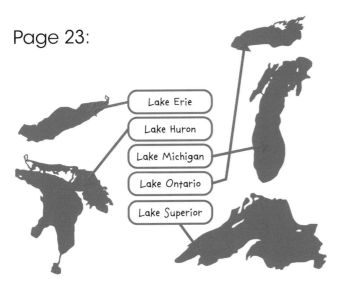

Lake Erie

Lake Huron

Lake Michigan

Lake Ontario

Lake Superior

Page 24: 1) Sledding, 2) skating, and 4) skiing would be fun to do on a glacier. Soccer would be too slippery!

Page 25:

the Arctic

Greenland

Places near the equator are hotter because they get the most direct sun.

the Antarctic

Page 26: a) worm and c) grasses

Page 27:

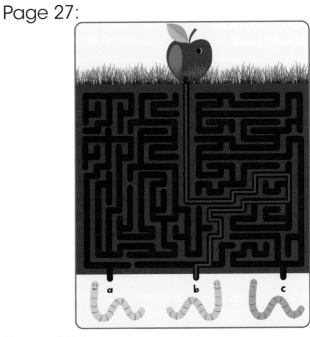

Page 29 top:

Page 29 bottom: SPRING and FALL

Page 30: The frog is in the tree.

Page 31: 1) a 2) c 3) b

Page 33 top:

Page 33 bottom:

Page 34: b) coal power

Page 36: You might find a, b, d, e, and f in the sky. You would not find an earthworm or an elephant in the sky.

Page 37: a) mesosphere b) troposphere c) thermosphere

Page 39 top: a) 4 b) 3 c) 1 d) 2

Page 39 bottom:

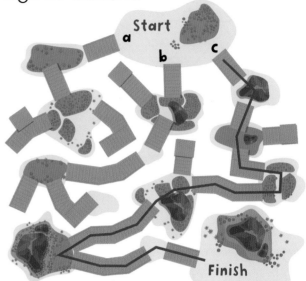

Page 41 top: The trench is 2.5 inches. The mountain is 1.5 inches.

Page 41 bottom: a) mountain b) lake c) valley d) river e) hill f) ocean. The seal is on a rock.

Page 43: You drew two feet walking.

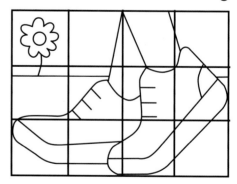

Page 44: 1) b - the crust 2) c - the Himalayas 3) b - They measure them from sea level. 4) d - all of these things 5) a - coal